MASHAM
MEANS EVENING

MASHAM
MEANS EVENING

KANINA DAWSON

COTEAU BOOKS

Edited by Elizabeth Philips
Designed by Tania Craan
Typeset by Susan Buck
Printed and bound in Canada at Imprimerie Gauvin

Library and Archives Canada Cataloguing in Publication

Dawson, Kanina, 1975-
        Masham means evening / Kanina Dawson.

Poems.
ISBN 978-1-55050-550-4

        1. Afghan War, 2001- --Poetry. I. Title.

PS8607.A962M38 2013   C811'.6   C2012-908199-X

Issued also in electronic format.

ISBN 978-1-55050-551-1 (PDF).--ISBN 978-1-55050-723-2 (EPUB).--
ISBN 978-1-55050-730-0 (MOBI)

        1. Afghan War, 2001- --Poetry. I. Title.

PS8607.A962M38 2013   C811'.6   C2012-908200-7

2517 Victoria Avenue
Regina, Saskatchewan
Canada S4P 0T2
www.coteaubooks.com

Available in Canada from:
Publishers Group Canada
2440 Viking Way
Richmond, British Columbia
Canada V6V 1N2

10 9 8 7 6 5 4 3 2 1

Coteau Books gratefully acknowledges the financial support of its publishing program by: The Saskatchewan Arts Board, including the Creative Industry Growth and Sustainability Program of the Government of Saskatchewan via the Ministry of Parks, Culture and Sport; the Canada Council for the Arts; the Government of Canada through the Canada Book Fund; and the City of Regina Arts Commission.

For my incredible daughter –
may you never be afraid to spill your coffee.

Love always, Mom.

CONTENTS

Kingston, *January 2007*

An itinerant sky is what's wrong –
its winds that shift and blow, its clouds that hang
in shades of grey over students sipping coffee,
their laughter and lofty sounding books crowding out my
    thoughts.
It's snowing. Everything smells of wet hem.

How this winter wears me out.

Watching others with their pocketed iPods, their trendy
suede boots, I notice I am not nearly stylish enough and that I
    text real slow,
like the growth of hair and nails.

Around me people study, they learn
linked head to head, or form a line to the cash like an isotherm.
Their smiles are all the same temperature.

I speak only to my coffee.

In it, the desert blinks. It sees me,
seizes me with its frayed rope –
the twine of old men made older by war,
binding each pomegranate in its crate.

I turn my face to the window. I go back.

I remember what it was
to feel alive in that place,
to do what mattered.

How under that sun, my skin,
like a husk of melon, was sweet.

Flights In

Weightless shake of plane keeps me awake.
In the semi-dark I hear the sound of soldiers sleeping,
involuntary legs afraid to be still,
heads lolling, the smack of chins falling
forward onto flak vests heavy as lead.
I keep my rifle tucked between my knees.

Farther down the row in the belly of the plane,
a couple of sergeants are reading with their helmet lamps on,
reminding me of home, of flashlights under the sheets
and my daughter, laughing
as she lit her face from beneath.

We made forts under the stairs.

At the airport she wouldn't let me go.
Eventually I had to hand her over, broken-
hearted, her limbs as limp as her damp hair.

How unfair
that I should think of this now,
desert-bound among the cargo netting and men,
our plane droning on, our wingtips flashing in the black
somewhere above the Gulf of Oman.

Landing in Kabul

We spend hours in the air, en route to Kabul.
I sleep until something like an impulse wakes me
and I know it's time to fumble for my helmet,
put my flak vest on.

A loadie moves through the dark, hand over hand
towards the back of the plane. He steps carefully
between our feet, a flashlight in his teeth.
He carries a pistol and something like an extension cord.
We are all roused from sleep.

There's a pause in the air, a slight downward shift
like we're tilting off a shelf, then I hear
the mechanical windings of our descent
and the plane falls into nothing I know.

I know it's not nothing, but still
I am shaken, weightless as we bank
left and right, up and down, avoiding
what lies below – mountains of the Hindu Kush
and shoulder-fired weapons.

My ears feel about to burst.

When we land it's night and I'm surprised
to see the lights of Kabul, twinkling, climbing the side of a hill
like Grouse mountain in Vancouver.

After the ramp comes down and I regain my feet,
I half-expect the sirens I hear
to be Vancouver City Police
moving through traffic in Granville.

The Road to Bagram

Horizons away from where I am going
we stop to change a tire on a road leading north.
It's littered with scrap metal, red and white painted rocks
telling us to be careful of mines.

Nearby is the faint clinking of goat bells
and the remnants of a checkpoint
where an Afghan guard is banging his pot against a metal post.

A speed bump in the middle of nowhere is what he tends to.
Long ago he might have kept a garden or read books.
Now he smokes hash and merely stares at us as we pass,
his AK slung, his kettle hung on a hook.

The wind makes a moan that cuts across the sun,
kicking up dust devils near an old Soviet tank
destroyed over a decade ago – its side ripped open,
its turret popped off and flung fifty feet

down a gravelled slope – nothing
history remembers. War came too many years ago,
scattered too many teeth among the rocks
where the goats now graze
and where the guard goes to take a shit –

uninterested in the lost jaw bone of some Russian
whose parents no one can name.

Souvenirs

An Afghan man is smoking something harsh,
sifting prayer beads through his hands,
giggling at my arms – bare but for a watch.

His teeth are dark like tarmac, like tobacco.
Or the heat I see shimmering in shades of brown
west of the mountains where he's from –
land of Massoud and pakol hats.

When the Soviets were here, he downed helicopters
and held freedom by the hip. All these years
he's managed to survive. Now in the shadow
of a post 9/11 airstrip, I browse the market,
buying bandoliers and Red Army badges,
his Soviet souvenirs.

Kabul University

The principal shows me in to her office
through a door that is cracked, punched
full of bullet holes.

Her heels click on the floor,
a post-Taliban luxury for a woman –
to make noise.

She serves us green tea with honey
in glasses that are chipped
and we ignore the smell of mildew
in the hallways as we sit – a smell like lamb's wool
left soured, sweating in the heat.

On the hills behind us, demining operations
shake the walls with the occasional controlled blast,
rattling the windows as we stir our tea, our spoons
trembling against glass. A rain of plaster
falls from the ceiling, but the principal doesn't flinch.
She barely bats an eye. Just smiles, amused,
at the dust in the air, at the pistol on my hip.

I can tell what she's thinking –
that this war is a mountain.
What good against it am I?

Some girls have gathered in the doorways to watch us.
Unveiled, they are giggling and graceful.
Outside it's a different story –
a wordless ushering of blue burqas, whispering
along the street, shuffling home in sandals, feet
the same colour as the dirt.

The principal tells us that even in Kabul
a girl can still lose her nose, her face,
her life, if she's not careful. If she doesn't stay
covered up. *You know*, she says, rising to shoo
boys away from her window, their hands
pressed against the pane, *we used to wear pants here.*

She smiles again, more sad this time,
and motions for me to come see the place outside
where last week an aid worker was shot to death
in a courtyard that used to be filled with flowers –
roses and rhododendron.

Earthquake at Camp Julien

Last week we were eating breakfast, Jess and I,
sitting in the tent while the cooks peeled potatoes,
when the world suddenly went dizzy. Our ears rang
and something wriggled underfoot. I told him
stop moving the table and he said he wasn't.
The light fixtures shook.

Later we would learn that an earthquake
had devastated parts of Pakistan, reaching
down into Kabul. That a dozen school girls
had died when their walls collapsed.

We felt bad, but we'd already been there awhile
and told ourselves how that kind of death
was better than being killed by Taliban.
They hated girls and killed them in ways
way worse.

So when the earthquake hit, Jess and I
didn't think in terms of loss. Instead
we told cock-sucking jokes from Team America
and spiralled out from the tent, laughing and falling,
weightless in our ignorance of what was to come
like passengers in a plane about to plummet.

Electoral Candidate

Woman in the Kabul marketplace
canvasses to jeers, the eyes
of her electoral photo gouged out.

Like a Taliban commander
she sleeps somewhere new
every night – letters

pinned to her door, telling her
to walk away or face rape
as reprisal.

Even her brothers say she'll only bring shame.

Together they decide
her fate for her instead –

to hold her down by the ears, to slit
her stomach until it grins.

It's a doctor who tells me this,
describing how he tried

to hold back her insides,
to plug her stomach
with his fist.

Knock-offs

In the ops room this morning I despised
the pile of pirated DVDs
recently acquired from the market
and Tim's new Rolex –
a knock-off that he bought
from an Afghan at the gate.

I hate how Tim told us
we're not here for altruism.
Then he looked right at me –
like I was some kind of liability
because yesterday at the airport,
I threw some kid a bottle of water
so he'd stop chasing our truck.
So maybe later he and his friends
wouldn't learn as fast to hate us
or take money for blowing us up.

Tim keeps talking about it.
He won't let it die.
When I try to tell him
there are two sides to every coin
he says – *drop it.* Then sighs
and spits chew into a cup.
You can't afford to be soft out here, he says.
You want them to get used to handouts?
He frowns and sets the time on his watch,
shaking his big bald head
as though I'm stupid.

July in Brishna Kot

Mid-afternoon and the sun presses down
against the back of my neck like one brick baking.

Mountains waver in the distance. The city flexes and folds.
From my place at the guard post I see the cemetery,
its belt of green flags bristling, standing on end
    among a million stones.
Motionless, except for one boy alone, walking home.

The sky is a sheath born hot. It collects the sweat
inside my helmet and gloves, along the inside of my legs –
the hot chafe, the salt stick of feeling like I just wet myself
is ever present.

This part of Kandahar is a hot moon.
A place where the dust goes up with each footfall
and every cleft in the rock becomes somewhere to escape the sun.
The markets are shuttered. The shops have all shut their eyes.
White is the only wise colour now.

Across the city, unexploded ordinance winds up like a ricochet,
waiting to hit the right note. A tuning fork, humming
    like instinct
in the back of my brain. I watch the boy
pick his way through the graves,
his days tied to a bomber's suicide like a timer
though neither of us can know it. It's already started to count back.

Like a leaf in the heat, like a bird in between blinks,
I keep still, listening for that tuning fork
its low note of caution, telling me
when time is up.

The Morning Commute

Driving through Kandahar City. Morning. 0730.
We've come straight from the airfield
and I'm holding a coffee, fresh
from the boardwalk.

There are goats to steer around.
A man stares.

Ah, says Christian. *The morning commute.*

I look down at my cup,
feeling ridiculously at ease.
Maybe I should get rid of this, I say,
taking another sip.

There are more goats. And two women in burqas,
hustling along. I catch the worry in the brown
flash of their heels like a sideways glance,
like maybe the rumours are true
and we're all rape-hungry Americans.

Why, asks Christian.
He drives carefully around them and waves – *Ladies.*

Even at this slow crawl we raise
dust clouds in our wake.

I don't know, I say, shrugging.
Because we're at war? It feels unprofessional.

Christian shrugs back.

So we hit an IED, he says.
*The worst that happens
is you spill your coffee.*

The White School House

This is what I learn from John in the ops room
on the morning of my day off – that dismounted patrols,
attempting to clear Taliban from among the rock walls
and grapevines west of Kandahar City, have been ambushed
near a school house.

The Taliban take three lives. Then they take one more
when an RPG slams into the side of an armoured carrier
on its way to the fight.

Later that day I learn that they are now in the midst
of falling back. Us – not them. It's surreal
to be told of this. Taliban in their flip flops
causing our 21st century war machines
to run backwards. *Back across the river,*

is how John puts it, pushing pins into a map
somewhere south of Arghandab – *To get us
the fuck out of there.*

Firefight

Attacks in the background,
beyond the outskirts of the city

become part of the nightly clutter of noise.
Inside the muffled tapping

of donkey hooves headed home, or boys
shouting, running their kites,

are the undertones of violence –

the *tock tock* of a Kandahar City police patrol
being ambushed on the road.

Consistent or sporadic, the sound of gunfire
varies but is constant –

a sound that instinct recognizes.

It filters into the subconscious
for later reference,

when we head out the gate.

Working for the Coalition

The Afghan cooks arrive at camp before dawn
so they don't get their heads cut off after work.

That can happen if they're not careful.

Last year an interpreter went missing from the airfield.
He was nabbed and taken away, hands holding him by the hair,
his heels left to kick, dragging in the dirt,
his throat slit.

The Taliban filmed it.

You can buy those DVDs in the city markets.
Powerful stuff, intimidation.

At the camp gate I watch as the cooks come shuffling in
one by one, laughing, arms raised.
They arrive in secret, filter in through the alleys.
Start peeling potatoes early.

You don't ask them where they live
or how big their families are or if the money's worth the risk.
You learn the odd word and point to what you want.
Sometimes they look confused. Mostly they grin,
sizing up our tattoos.

It's amazing the things you don't stay amazed at. Afghan cooks
risk losing their heads to make rice with lamb and eggplant,
    something
none of us even like.

The Wrong Crowd

Before you were used as a Taliban sentry in these hills,
before you were a bone, blown apart
    and lodged in the rock of this cave,
before the geckos found you and made nests of your skull,
you were not necessarily against the West.

Maybe you just fell into step with the wrong crowd, got recruited
from a refugee camp on the border, somehow hoping to be reborn
or maybe just make a buck. After all, the Madrassas
    can only take so many
and your mother had other children to feed. You used to be
    one of those
typical kids from the camp, wearing a donated sweater
    with a leaf pattern
and too-short sleeves. Constantly wiping your nose on them. Kind
until you learned not to be.

Maybe I'm naive. Maybe I want you to be something more
than what people say you are – an opium-smoking
religious faggot. A product of the buggery
    you must have asked for
in order to keep watch from this rock face. Not much liked,
but still used all the time, you took the grunting of old men
behind a pigeon-laced wall at noon.

At night your Taliban brothers would have made supper,
laughing at the fact that they wouldn't be the first ones found
if the Americans stormed this place. It would be you –
up on the rock cliff, struggling to take a shit –

your eyes wet with yawning, your lungs remembering
what it was to run through camp with a plastic bag kite
in boots too big for your feet, the taste of smoke
from your mother's cooking fires and all the things

you had to eat – before the bad choices –
naan bread with rice and chicken,
sometimes saffron.

Once you had a soccer ball.
And a name –

Abdul-Hanaan, slave
of the merciful.

Repatriation and a Rainstorm

Shot down over the northern edge of Kandahar, he is repatriated
back to Ontario on a day of thunderstorms. Air smelling of rain
and weedy-bottomed lakes. The pressure of clouds
like a steep descent.

Onlookers line the streets, waiting in the wind for his plane to land
in two-star Trenton, the leaves of each tree
turning inside out.

As the crowd stands hushed, looking
    for that grey fin of plane to appear,
his family files out onto the tarmac, holding on to their hats,
    each other
as though they are old.

I recall that photo of him, the one that gets taken
before you go overseas – the same day you get all your needles
and anti-malarial pills.

He was one of the few to have smiled.

You never think it's going to be you.

Helicopter Crash

Crumpled, dusty, whirling into the camp wall,
a helicopter folds, burning like a metal deck of cards,
melting the seatbelts.

No way to get them out, the pilot and door gunner.
Inside the operations centre the order gets given –
start making the calls back home.

The officer in charge swallows hard, nods.
Poised on the last step of the stairs
he feels his own bones on fire,
thinks of his boys, eleven and thirteen, says –
It would be quick though.
It would be quick.

But I can tell from his face –

how he sees those flames
like a tableau, those hands
in a cockpit spasming for air –

that he's not sure.

The General's Briefing

The briefing room smells like a cottage
closed up in the dead of summer
or a second-hand shop in July.

We are sticking to our chairs, Sean and I,
listening to a fan that makes noise, but moves no air.

We have a few minutes to wait.

The General is at a ramp ceremony –
an American this time, and one of Hannah's friends.
Died in her arms in Pashmul.

She told me this on the boardwalk at KAF,
out front of the Tim Horton's trailer
and I said that I was sorry for her loss. Us Canadians
were holding steady at twenty-three. I wondered
what number it was for them. A shitty thing
to keep track of, even worse to lose it.

The door to the briefing room opens, closes. A thousand times
I twist the cap on a water bottle warm as a beach.

We go over our notes.

Outside the plane takes off and I start to feel sad.

Then the General brushes in and it's all business.
He takes his seat, apologizing
for being late.

Casting the Net

Dirty, fecal, filled with old fruit skins and farts,
the canal breaks the city in half, one side full of bad guys –
quiet, watchful, arms clasped behind their backs
(no booms there – they don't shit in their backyard)
and the other side, full of merchants, the maybe not-so-bad guys
where the booms go off instead, amid spice carts
and propane stands,
schoolgirls and us.

We're getting ready to roll into this mess, paused, idling at the gate.
Inside our truck I turn my head against the heavy stink of air
trying to avoid that shit taste it leaves on the tongue.
A pair of leather gloves is broiling on the dashboard.
The burning outline of a sun, reflected on the ground
in puddles full of algae scum.

The radio crackles with reports of troops in contact, under fire
somewhere southwest of the city, where last night I watched
bonfires on the hill and wondered what they meant. Guessing
gets old when nothing in this desert is news. I ache to discern
something concrete, something definitive that I can use
to turn the tide of this thing.

Listening to troops locked in a firefight, the driver
looks out over the canal, the endless sprawl
　　of clay-coloured compounds.
He eyeballs an old Afghan man who is eyeballing us.

Says he wishes we had found a more reliable way
to tell the bad from the not-so bad,
the everyday man from the Taliban –
none of this one-by-one shit.

I imagine looking down on the city. I envision it
like a picture from the top. Us in the middle
spreading out our nets, draining these compounds like a sea
until all that's left are Taliban, conveniently marked, caught
flopping on the bottom. The shock of air
hitting their gills like a jackboot.

When the gate goes up it yanks my thoughts
    back into the truck. We roll out
past the old Afghan man – *older than dirt* the driver says
and we laugh, scanning the streets for suicide bombers –
    that stillness,
that telltale lingering, those quiet signs of hate
like ripples in the water – bottom feeders
humping the muck for their dinner, hiding
deep among the everyday weeds.

Shades of Grey

Spores of metal are in this Afghan man like a blood smell,
his hand stump wrapped in gauze, his lower legs full of pins.

He keeps his face turned to the hospital wall
and I see his throat work hard at swallowing –
a dry well.

I hear he got injured when his plough struck a mine.
But the medics on call say – *Don't let him suck you in.*
We see this all the time. He's no farmer.

The man moves a blanket with his stump.
Runs his tongue around the metal
anaesthetic taste of his mouth.

He moans that he wants to be released.
Says, please – he has a family to care for
and his plough is what hit the mine.

But the medic, familiar with wounds, is unconvinced
and thinks he knows how most of this man's hand has gone –
on a night with no moon, in hushed and hurried digging,
    emplacing
roadside bombs.

Incoming

A few of us stand outside in the compound, a moment spent
in quiet camaraderie, looking up, losing thought,
the fat moon a full cow bawling in the sky –

then something goes whizzing by
in the dark overhead, uncategorized.

I know what it is. Not fast enough though.

A high, falling whistle fills the night eye and my brain
is stuck open like the aperture of a pinhole camera
capturing each upside-down frame

a split second before impact, instinct
screaming at us to move, like bull riders
storing curse words in the mouth for later,

too late to be of use.

We are halfway to our rooms
when a dark, hurtling star drives us all to ground,
fumbling for sudden cover, the giant bang of its boom
leaving us open-mouthed in the dust.

Soft Things

Escaping the confines of the office, Todd takes a smoke break
out back where some Afghan workers are digging a ditch.
They squat behind their shovels and shade their eyes,
sucking on their scarves to keep moisture in their mouths.

Yesterday we lost two more guys to an IED –
not the fault of Afghans in general, but these ones
keep their distance, knowing we're angry enough
to blame them anyway.

Plus it's hot. And we're all getting on each other's nerves.

When Todd returns he lets the screen door bang behind him.
It's the third time that day and Sean sighs, rolling his eyes.
Todd announces that he's seen a kitten outside – an event –
because things here don't thrive.

My roommate runs, clapping her hands for something soft.
She can't wait to hold it. Her mouth is an *Ohhhhh*.
All week she has been alone in her head, tossing at night,
nervous and afraid to dream. Afraid the next IED
will be hers.

She hurries outside and the screen door slams.
Don't forget your purse, Todd jokes.
I watch his shoulders go up and down.
There is a pause in the sound of shovels
ringing against the rocks in the dirt
as the Afghans stop to watch.

Todd says, laughing –
Guess I should have told her it was dead.
Through the screen door I see
her hands fall, her face
go the colour of Vanilla Bean body cream.

An Awning of Birds

Waiting for a convoy to come in,
an Afghan policeman with his AK slung,
hot hush of slippers on his feet, beckons me
to where guards gather for yogurt
in the garden beneath a tree, alive
with little brown sparrows, an awning of birds.

He wants to show me their latest prize –

a car his men have just towed in, a white Saracha,
bullet-holed, its windows broken,
the driver side door streaked with blood.
Air fresheners from Iran hang, slowly
turning above the dash.

This bomber they shot – before he went off.

I wish I could ask how they knew
to be so sure – if it was just luck or something else,
something in the way he moved behind the wheel
that lacked peace. The forehead sweat, the glimpse
of gritted teeth.

Across the city an echo reverberates in the air
like the rumbling of an earthquake, dispelling
the men from their afternoon shade. Disturbed,
the birds lift as one flock from the tree.

The policeman looks at me and grins. *Boom*, he says,
then motions for me to take his picture, posing
in the garden with his knife drawn, while beyond the wall
birds circle and sirens begin.

Friendly Fire

Section commander, stranded, soaked in his seventh hour of battle
dismounts in the vineyards near Pashmul, his vehicle bogged down

in the irrigation ditch – having just taken incoming fire,
      having just lost two of his crew
to blood wounds he couldn't tourniquet.

He radios for air strikes against the enemy. Coalition firepower
takes to the skies above them, only to miss by half a click. He listens

to the five-hundred-pounder they drop
come whistling in towards him.

Shouts at what's left of his men to get down,
tastes dirt, feels heat, plugs one ear and thinks

Shit –
this one's gonna be close.

Little Bird

Headed down a dirty side street after a rain,
mud churns under our tires.
Ratty-edged rugs are hung out to dry
in alleys where chickens roam, pecking the dirt,
and boys jostle each other to spit
at our truck as we drive by.

Then a small girl emerges, like a tiny brown bird.
She ducks shyly out from behind a wall. We wave
and she waves back – her sudden grin, bright as a bare bulb
amid those boy-filled alleys, her brothers hooting with sticks,
her uncles squatting to take a piss. They glare and wipe their feet
when they're done, the way cats bury their shit.

Too late, I realize our mistake. This isn't Kabul –
you don't wave at girls here
even if you are one.

In the truck's mirror as we pass, an uncle
removes his shoe and brings it down on her
again and again, her feet twisting in the dirt,
her dusty flutter of hands clutching
at her head, her dress
green as grass.

Medics on their Break

They shouldn't smoke, but need to –
medics on their break

out by the runway or under the few trees
using smoke as some kind of expression

for what's been done, lived, breathed.

Smoke as some kind of memory
that can be expelled through the mouth.

Their little hurt curls of thought
drifting out across the city –

the dissipate of loss.

Heavy

Witnessing the remains of another soldier
offloaded at Camp Mirage is the contracted mortician
from McKinnon and Bowes, and the camp's chief firefighter.

They don't go to the morgue until after supper.
It's dark and hot. The stars
are small and still.

On the tarmac a plane, its cargo discharged,
is docking for the night – isolated
lights out on the runway
reminiscent of ships at sea.

The mortician dabs at his head with the end of his tie,
then takes it off and stuffs it in his pocket
as he walks. There are sweat patches
on his armpits and crotch.

A truck is backed, beeping
into its bay. A chain link fence
rattles. Footsteps in the gravel
beyond the gate. The lights
go on in the morgue.

The mortician and the firefighter arrive
with the necessary paperwork, waiting
to be let in.

Then someone opens the door.
It's infinitely heavy.

At first there's a whirlwind
in their mouths. That silent,
vacuuming suck in which nothing

can survive – not words, not sound.

Then the knowledge
that what must have been a terrible violence
is somehow gone, inexplicably leaving

as though tossed on a shore –
this body.

Fishing for Taliban

To find them I must dream the way fish do, hovering
just above the bottom in the deeper parts of the water,

unblinking, with only the occasional
fanning of my fins to keep me still.

I must dream of hiding places. I must dream the origins
of these insurgents like a birth place or a food source
to which they instinctively return.

Everything I know is inhaled through my skin
and my eyes never close.

When I swim it will be upstream, quietly gliding
side to side, mouthing the water for their smell.

Optics

The dead are supposed to be made bare
by their nothingness. Made more human
in succumbing. Their bodies stripped of myth.

But this man – a Talib – dead of an airstrike,
was something other than that, something
from a comic strip – the antagonist
who gets what he deserves and the word
SHAZZAM written in jagged letters
above his head.

He sat where the blast had thrown him
upright against a rock, head flattened
like a paper beak, privates exposed.

Still, I keep coming back to his face,
his head caved in, his one eye
blooming like a spyglass –

a telescopic pearl that if given the chance
might have predicted my future.

On the Wall

Forearms resting on the wall of the camp perimeter
with its trip flares and plastic bagged barbed wire,
I spit pomegranate seeds and watch birds among the rafters
of a guardhouse, their beaks sucking heat from the shade.

The mountains are amber in the early afternoon sun. I squint
across the city, put one of them in between my finger and thumb.
I'm not supposed to be up here – at least not without a gun
    or a uniform on.

A breeze kicks up and I lean out, exposed. Locals on the road
stare up at my t-shirted arms and my falling down hair.
    I don't care.
For once I am huge, my hand the span of a mountain.

Down below in the gravel compound, James wanders by
on his way to get lunch, long-legged and disparaging,
his pistol hung from his hip. He yells –

What the fuck are you doing up there?
You wanna get your mother-fuckin' head blown off?

Start of the Rainy Season

I remember a bombing in which a civilian
riding in a military convoy had been killed,

his truck tumbling over concrete barriers
and into shop fronts made from sea cans.

The rain had made everything slick
and afterwards, no one knew whose legs were whose –

somehow the medics had ended up with extras.

I heard all of this later
from the soldiers who were there.

One of them spat in the dirt.
Shook his head. Shrugged.

He told me how they always had to fight
to get this guy to wear his flak vest and helmet.

Fuckin' civilians, he had said
as though he couldn't afford to care.

After that,
the rain just kept coming.

Drowning in a Kharez

Someone has drowned out there – in a kharez.

What the hell is a kharez? Brian wants to know.
John launches into a description, but my brain stalls,
stuck on the shit show that this is. Drowning –
in a desert well of all things. How the world must have fallen away.
He would have been there – walking – and then suddenly gone
like the swoosh of a garbage chute, boots bent backwards,
kit clanging down the sides of a rock wall.

Jesus, he might have said.

Then maybe his vacancy would have reached a place
in the back of someone's head – muffled water burps
like a far off fish jumping on an evening pond –
and the mad scramble would have begun
on hands and knees across the rock face, frantically
feeling the ground for an opening of some sort.

Rope – someone yelled. *I need fucking rope.*
Get me some rope up here now. Then in the dark,
punctuated by the plink of gravel being kicked over an edge,
his men thundered in towards that hole,
sweat shaken from their eyes, flashlights gripped in their teeth.

Get him the fuck out.

From down below they blocked out the sky.
Stars obliterated by the shapes of men crouched at a mouth.
Brian is disgusted. By which part I don't know.
All of it, probably. We all are. Quiet
and hanging our heads. We want him back.

Jesus, John – Brian says, kicking a door, then a desk –
*Why couldn't you just have said
it was a well.*

Killed by a Suicide Bomber, *December 6*

Big man – Floridian – don't think you don't know him.

Wears suspenders and a t-shirt – is tall,
talks constantly,

works private security on a highway half-built
thanks to war.

Says he's been here for a year. Says proudly
how no one but him

has been to Panjwayi – in jeans.

He counts his near misses. Throws back his head
like a horse when he laughs.

Drinks coffee with me and swears

he won't change for them.

Driftwood

I heard you were from B.C.

I heard how they fought for you
in the back of the armoured carrier,
telling you to breathe.

The driver's intercom was on.
The medics that brought you in bit back tears
at the sound of your guys counting along
with compressions that just wouldn't work.

In the hospital hall they swept you past me.
You were shirtless, your head wrapped
as though protected from sound, but I'm sure there was some
still eddying boom inside the aftermath that was you.

Later we remarked how that whole scene
had smelled like a barn, and how a photographer
had stuck his arm through the door to take pictures.

We all hated that.

Then someone said *Come on.*
We got more wounded.
And we did, we had four –

but the worst part was overlooking
the small details of your death, your body
heavy as an ocean, your feet
rolling

back and forth on that stretcher
like logs on a west coast beach.

Dangerous Men

I remember a village in which we sat,
the local men and us, a tiny gathering on a grass patch
bleached by the daily dump of night urine,
salty hot. I sat with my back against a fire brick wall,
sweet with smoke and crawling with flies.

The men there had laughed at my hair,
used their hands to scoop the insides out of melons,
taught me words for bird and trees and sky.

We were offered apricots, the hospitality of almonds
and we talked about the price of peace.

We didn't know until later how dangerous
these men were, pretending to be friends of the coalition,
covering our hands with both of theirs, smiling,
letting our trucks return home in the semi-dark, unmolested.

We thought that meeting a great success.

Back in Canada we figure it out – what duplicity means –
when we hear that one of our own got his head cleaved with an axe.
He'd been sitting among the elders, sipping tea and spitting seeds
when someone slumped him into darkness.
Made of him a melon, split,
halved.

They hoped it would be enough to make us leave.

And I remember how I'd sat not six months before
in a place like that, laughing, cross legged on the ground,
my helmet off, my grimy tea glass resting against one knee –
the men with their sticky hands, sucking their fingers clean,
telling us how their district was famous for its melons,
its hospitality.

Hearing from God

I'm off by myself, stealing moments in the shade of a wall,
thumbing through books and last year's magazines,
celebrity pregnancies that have come and gone, perfume samples
ripped from the seams. Things from another life.

Then you arrive, restless and disgruntled,
talking shit about your ex-wife –
how she's *fucking crazy,* how the sex was no good,
how she won't move out of your place.

It's all trivial compared to our larger hurts –

like the four we just lost in Panjwayi.
We won't know who they are until the next of kin
take over the dead and the news finally names a face.
Only then do we really know.

It's a dread that grips the camp.

When the medevac choppers pass overhead
and the medics abandon their breakfast, sadness
strikes me, not just because of our injured –
inbound on the helipad, broken-backed and struggling to breathe –

but because you're still holding down my books,
shouting above the page flap and rotor din
that your ex is a kook, telling you she won't leave
until she hears from God.

Fawns

An IED goes off and two of our guys get hit,
in a convoy moving south
back to the airfield.

We are dispatched to go get them –
Ben and Big Carl.

It's a crazy night drive.

Our trucks race through the vacant city streets, full of dust.
Above us an American gunship circles, looking for prey,
its instruments trained on the road.

I'm afraid that in the dark far below,
the pilots might mistake us
for something else.

When we finally get to the scene it's all hell and Big Carl waves.
There's dark on his shirt and Ben shakes his head
as though there's water in his ear.

There are headlights. A helicopter
sends dust into my mouth.
We load everyone up.

I try to drive easy, but the feel of the boom
keeps the deafened boys in the back
nervous and bracing at every invisible bump,
their hands pressed up against the roof.

The guys tell me they're okay, but every time I look
at their new-fawn sweaty hair and torn sleeves
it's like a shock of air to the newly born, a sharp hoof.

Flights out of Howz-e Madad

Some of our guys get medevacked back to camp,
heads wrapped in gauze, their femurs packed tight,
field dressings soaked through.

They had taken casualties – a few of them –
somewhere west of the mountains
and had to be extracted,

the chopper barely able to touch down –
too much incoming fire.

Finally they have everybody on, shuddering, strapped in,
the wounded lying nose to nose.

Beneath the *whump whump* of the rotor blades straining to be gone,
medic scrambles to start IVs.

Once they're in the air, pilot says to co-pilot –
You got anything to eat?

He balances altitude with food, downs chicken fingers
stained brown with cold ketchup.

Bringing the chopper out around the backside of the mountain,
pilot glances over his shoulder at medic fighting to find a vein

then shouts above the deafening
pulse of rotor blades turning –

How's it going back there?

Man from Uruzgan

An Afghan man hangs around outside our gate.
The things he says may or may not be believed,
his one glass eye fixed on my hand, a bird
out of bread.

My brother is dead, he says.
The Taliban took him.

The guard at the gate swears he just wants cash,
but we let him in anyway, into a room
smelling of old ass, the couch stinking of sweat.

The gate guard asks him what he knows,
but the man just shrugs, looks down at his toes –
tells us how he came all the way from Uruzgan.

He wants a cigarette, the first step
in a timeless game called give.

He wiggles a tooth, coyly
as though sweetening the deal, and says –

The Taliban tried to take me too

but then
they let me live.

Death Like Divorce

Seven in one blow. And what a blow.
A bomb so big the undercarriage of their vehicle
cracked like a tooth gone bad.

Recovery, like a harvest,
gets done by the light of the moon.

At the airport the loadies have a tough time of it,
but so does everyone – carting the bodies off to cold storage,
first one desert, then the next – a long, slow line
breaking everyone's backs.

In Camp Mirage the bathroom stalls get etched with graffiti;
names and dates, the occasional anti-war slogan.
As if the wogs in Mirage know anything about it, we say, uncaring.

I stay up for tea and watch the stars gutter out, one by one.

Beside me on the makeshift patio, the padré
in between phone calls and on his fourth cup of coffee,
runs a hand through his hair and smiles.
He is careful not to sigh.

Death, like divorce,
must be kept from the kids.

Omar

Some myth. So they say he lost an eye
fighting the Russians. A lot of them did.

His gardeners hated him – and the newest wife,
the one with the room painted rare as raw meat,
was the first to lose a son in the bombing, hidden
optimistically in tunnels that Omar had built.

How their ears must have burst when it caved
beneath that American cavalcade – dust and dead geckos
flung from the walls, wives stumbling
beneath their burqas, the smell of rosewater and onion
on their breath since breakfast.

After that they all left – Omar and his crew,
late that night on a highway through Arghandab –
doubled up on motorbikes, one wife
burning her leg on the exhaust.

In the rush to abandon Kandahar,
Omar left his Land Cruisers and a cow behind.

But before all that, wifeless on a rooftop –
acne scarred, a nobody,
forgotten at night and swept by stars –
I wonder, was he one-eyed, or not?

Mass Murder and a Dog Fight

The boom goes up from behind a break in the mountains
and boys, stomping a cat to death in the cemetery, stop.

In the rock, an echo or two gets trapped,
funnelled up the valley. Bone splinters of noise
like a fractured rocket whistle. Then a gradual silence –
like driving away from a beach.

It is some time before the sirens happen
way south in the city.

We watch from along the wall,
off duty with our elbows hanging over,
wondering who bought it.

This time it's civilians at a dog fight –
at least a hundred of them –
and Arghandab's Chief of Police.

Wanting him dead, the Taliban
detonated their Datsuns in the crowd.

It had been the first time in a long time
that civilians had felt safe enough to gather,
laughing, pitting dog against dog
in the Arghandab valley.

Their echoes were caught and held
like an empty seashell,
something now void of a home –

the yelping of dogs cut
short, the cheering of boys and men
blown out of their shoes.

Life on a Forward Operating Base

Hunkered down, pinned
sometimes for hours, getting shelled at night
by the enemy's makeshift mortars, harassed
so that sleep never comes –

troops on an isolated forward operating base
west of Kandahar City joke about how they're fine
as long as the smokes don't run out.

They get rotated back through the airfield
every few weeks so the guys get a break,
but life still reads like a laundry list

– get hit, chopper out the wounded,
make it back to camp.

Same thing
month after month.

The comforts of home
slowly diminish,

mortars keep coming –

on the roof
someone writes

Send Smokes.

Embedded

Sticking to my chair in the camp's tiny welfare room,
shoulder to shoulder with troops surfing the net or calling home,
I read the online paper, greedy for news – another point of view
to show me something of this place from the outside looking in.

What I read is disappointing, leaves me cold, diffused.
An article about a Pakistani journalist
giving interviews to the Taliban,
sipping tea for a story, watching ambushes unfold.

It only takes a moment for me to run my thoughts
like a skewer through the back of every armoured carrier
that's seen its hull cracked, its seats torn apart, witness marks
left in dark red on the ceiling. This was someone's heart.

If I had a picture, I could point to the facts.

They were here and here and here, when they landed –
those soldiers that got caught in that IED attack,
flung hard, like something coming off the top
of a violent spin cycle.

And here is where the armour on their carrier gave out.
And here are their water bottles and ration packs
and foil wrappers and bits of burnt kit strewn about.

And here is the shit culvert that they didn't spot –
the little pile of rocks disguising jerry cans and command wires
that lead back through the grapevines.

And farther up on the ridgeline overlooking all this
the Pakistani journalist and his Taliban hosts
would have stood, watching a Canadian convoy
approach in the distance, raising dust clouds a mile long.

Panjwayi

Four more soldiers died today – dismounted,
handing out children's things in Panjwayi.

A bicycle bomber
pedalled past and detonated,
taking children with him.

Fuck, Joe says when I tell him.

Fuck Fuck Fuck

If he'd been wearing a hat
he would have thrown it down.

I stare up at the sky.

Joe spits on the ground.

Some of his closest friends
were out there.

Not Wasting Time on Griefs that Don't Matter

I make friends with a girl from another camp.
Her room is nicer than mine, stacked with books
and hung with scarves – beautiful curtains to nowhere.

No windows because there might be mortars,
but there's a vodka bottle hidden in one corner
beneath a heap of laundry she hasn't had time to do
and her bed with the duck down comforter
hasn't seen much use.

She calls it her battlespace – a place to wage war.
On afternoons when I was in camp, she'd hand me her keys
on the way out the door, red hair flying
telling me to make myself at home.

I used to wonder what she could possibly find to fight
in darkness that soft.

Then I learn this week she lost a friend and last month a lover.
They were both so out of the blue, she says. *I had to choose
who to grieve. One got hit in his truck
and the other* – here she shakes her head, shrugs –

sent me a fucking letter.

She tells me it was a no-brainer, that she can't waste time
on the griefs that don't matter. But it still doesn't cover
the fact that nothing out here is ever gradual.

Whether it comes in the mail or explodes on the road
our hearts go hurtling forward inside the wreckage
long after everything else has stopped.

Halfway House

I think of it as a halfway house – Camp Mirage –
a place between war and home
where we write letters and wear shorts
and watch outdoor movies from our lawn chairs
in the sand of the volleyball court. Guys make jokes
    about Afcrackistan.
At the Canex we buy new sheets in which to sleep
and Dubai silverware to send home because it's cheap.
There's even a bus that will take you to the Emirates mall.
If you're lucky you'll see the camel jockeys
on their tracks of sand, racing alongside the highway
and the stable boys carrying tea to the powerful, perfumed sheikhs,
their white dish-dash flapping in the breeze.
All this, as you find your way to the souk
to buy pearls
or a ring.

Also at the halfway house
between war and home, the bodies come temporarily to rest,
bumping down in their soundless metal isolation, offloaded,
then the plane refuels. The pilots hunch tiredly over tea.
The loadies stand out on the runway, gloved
    and smothered by heat.
It's a different desert for them. Not opulent, but removed.
They get what's leftover.
They get the dead.

Seasons in Kandahar

I'm sitting near the runway, a place of grace and great thumps,
watching aircraft come hurtling in and out,

watching heat lines recede, bleeding sunset
into rows of willow trees dry as a furnace.

The air smells fungal with sewage and old November –
how supper comes across on the tongue, pungent

as meat pie. The pilots line up to eat –
or send someone to get it.

Hunkered on a bench, hands hugging a cold cup of coffee,
I watch as heat fades from the day and the crows fly
away from the fast food trailers on the boardwalk, repatriated
back to their mountains.

Beyond the mechanical wind-up of rotors
lifting medevac crews into the air, my eyes hold them going –
a line of ragged black dots on the horizon.

Self Immolation

When there is no voice but this. Fire. Lit
with a kerosene fuelled spark. As if to say –
Watch me. It flares up
from her feet, then engulfs
her heart, frantically
beat out by her mother
before it reaches her face.

The hospitals here are unequipped.
Her sisters have gathered, wailing
in the hallways, their children clinging
to their legs. Her mother sits, slumped
against the wall.

There's nothing the doctors can do.

This morning when they brought her in
she cried out in agony, her hands a crazy spasm,
fingers melted to the bone.

Now she is whimperless, alone on her bed.
Breathing through a piece of muslin
wet as wet leaves, she will take
twenty-four hours to die.

Life in a Cemetery

Graveyards in Kandahar –
not the same as they are back home.
Not manicured and full of flowers, but dusty,
shallow, heaped up, full of stones.

If you die a martyr here, a flag – either green or white –
will flutter, torn on a pole near the rocks at your head
until the constant flap of wind
pulls it loose.

Strangers will come and call you brother, or uncle.
Prayers will be said and your scarves will be re-hung,
your grave place decorated with pieces of salt
said to cure ailments and infertility –
you're that holy.

Women will put these pieces of you under their tongue.

Children will go there, to your cemetery
to chase or stone cats, to make a dog drop
whatever it is he is carrying away.

You'll hear the Jingle Trucks on the road, their horns
like something stripped from a carnival
and bursts of gunfire, meaning
either marriage or death.

At night young men will stroll past your feet,
giggling, eyes lined with kohl,
and disappear among the myriad
stone mounds, holiness forgotten.

If you had eyes left to open, you'd see them through the dark
by the graves at your feet, caught up in each other,
green-eyed like racoons, feet shoulder width apart.

The Only Chair in the Room

My roommate is a lesbian.
Dark-haired, with a Newfie's grin.
Don't ask, don't tell, the guys say, laughing
as I head in through my door.

Sometimes she makes my bunk for me
and when I'm out, worries
that I might not be back, and when I am, worries
over whether or not I'll be warm enough at night.

She loans me her spare quilt and shares all the junk food
from the care packages that she gets.
Samantha-sends-them-like, she says.
Her accent makes it sound like all one word.

The guys poke fun and ask what it's like
to shower with one. *One what?* I say,
knowing exactly what they mean.
I don't tell them she's more modest than me
or that a long time ago she used to date a guy
who just died from an RPG strike in that last firefight.
She cried her eyes out that day.

Or how the other night when the rockets came flying in
        we happened to trap
some sort of ridiculous, hairless mouse on sticky paper
and how that was the thing that made us both run shrieking,
        helmets on,
for the only chair in the room.

Dust Storm at Kandahar Airfield

We are walking up the road at the airfield, Christian and I,
as though walking off the edge of the world
one tent at a time – huddled, stooped against the wind,
our scarves fluttering, tattered
like the edges of flags.

A minute ago it was afternoon.
Now a god-like fist of dust and sand
has clenched daylight off at the heart.

Ahead, Canada House appears in the gritty gloom,
dome-like, a lonely ark where troops filter out in ones and twos
past the foosball tables and cigarette butt cans,
their smokes in hand.

They've just held another memorial.

We go in, half-blind, to the smell of hot chocolate,
our faces stiff with dirt.

The atmosphere is hushed.
Of all the fucking luck, someone says.
I step aside. Let the troops file by
and out into the dust.

The canvas flap falls behind me,
cutting out the sound of wind, the sight
of tiny white lights swinging
wildly between the tents – a far string of stars
tossed on a whirlwind.

Forecast

Wind wakes me this morning.
The sound of a door banging –
open, closed. Open, closed.
Outside a grey stretch of clouds
hangs over the city. There's rain
and more bombings.

It's the Taliban's winter push for superiority
and lately the forecast has been the same –
cold wet wind and suicide fires,
ash mixed into rain.

Dangling my feet off the edge of my bunk,
I keep my blankets wrapped around my shoulders
and wish for something gentler than what the day is sure to bring –
the threat of metal, driven, exploded into stone.

I wish we could tunnel under
this weather, mole-like – burrow
far beneath the trees, unseen
into milkweed-feathered nests.

Then those blood and rain puddles
held captive in the craters
of Kandahar's shitty main road
would be far above us, and the mess –

the asphalt memory of yesterday's boom
that got buried in that soldier's knees and face
like a shattered dinner plate –
would be several stratum away,

mistaken by us in our dry, deep holes
for nothing more than the rumbling
of an inconsequential thunder.

Disconnected

We drive by the remains of a suicide bomber –
his hair a bloody ruff held aloft by a policeman.

He is proud to have found it, like a mutt
shaking out the prize of his mane.

I was sunk deep within myself, thinking of my daughter
swinging her bucket in the rain on the way to the compost heap,

and me – married, steeped, hip deep in the green fields of home
when I saw the hole where the bomber's face should have been.

Its oval of open bone endings, jaws
pried apart.

My heart jolted, involuntary
as a tongue running over a loose tooth.

For a moment I was that bloody space –
that bundle of raw nerves where the air hits and makes pain.

I thought about how this man was born
the same as any man I've known.

The policeman grins as we pass,
shoving the head into a bag, and I am torn

between worlds –

my daughter at home in her bare feet, scattering
eggshells and ash

and this bombed out vehicle to my right,
a popping metal fire

where they keep finding teeth.

Taliban

I am one of the faithful. I live among those
who line their eyes with kohl, who skim the top
off the opium crop, giggling when we get caught
behind a compound wall, our pants pulled down,
a boy in our mouth. I learn what I've been taught –
to sting the invaders until they are stunned.
It is what God has provisioned.

Commanders tell us that our past is glorious –
a blazing line of sacrifice –
and that our future will be rewarded.

They tell us war is when we rest in God. But we're still young.
Sometimes we quake, our hands shaking in the aftermath.
We bury what dead we can, stealing their sandals
then rubbing eggplant on our wounds. Taking opium at noon
in the secrecy of the vineyard, I numb
my own fear. When I close my eyes
I can't be seen.

When the shock of war wears off we brag
about our ability to vanish into villages, silently
reciting the Arabic history of words we'd never heard
until Al Qaeda came.

At night we name the invaders, invoking
longwinded and passionate phrases
about how we'll kill them. When darkness falls
we huddle up, hungry, holding hands,
long bones of cold woven within our interrupted sleep.
In the morning we eat grapes off the ground.

When the helicopters come we run or lie still –
anything to avoid their guns. Even in the dark

they can make your body fly apart, your mouth
open without sound. The same thing we crave
for the invaders, may we prick them
according to what is promised.

Support is drummed up on the dust of our heels,
our governance given in the form of ultimatums,
the blood of teachers, the measurement of beards.
Shame on you if you're split between the legs –
you women, keep your foulness hidden – still,
your fear is what fascinates. If I got you alone
I'd jab my fingers into the damp centre of that pain.

Education is irrelevant. We praise God without it.
Insist on this so-called right and we'll marry you
to dirt. Bloodshed is what sells to the illiterate
in the marketplaces of Afghanistan. I stroll
through the city at will, my hands clasped
behind my back. My newness gone,
my turban black.

A Night in Hospital

A Taliban fighter, staring, drugged,
dragged wounded from the desert fight,
hangs his head against the bed and won't look away.
He touches himself while I turn my back
and fake sleep on my side.

I shut my eyes.

Drinking is hard. Fluid drips from an IV hooked to my arm.
Rustle and pump beneath the covers, I hear the Talib
and his one free hand getting a slow start on himself
until a medic walks by and yells –

Knock that shit off.

Fever comes and goes, then night falls for us all.
Little Afghan girl in the far corner, caught
in the same fight as the Taliban, whimpers,
clutching her stomach wound and donated doll.

All I have is appendicitis.

Lying there, feeling dumb, no choice
but to listen and wait for the medics to come
    give her another dose,
I try to steel myself against her voice, thin as soup,
to keep balanced on the knife edges of sleep.

But the visuals keep running a loop –

that Taliban fighter, cuffed one-handed in the bed to my right.
He fixes my face in his emaciated gaze. Jackknifing
beneath the sheets, he gets himself off, then drools
blood into a bucket.

Ahmadullah's Toes

The only tree in the garden of the camp is auditory –
full of birds, and hot smelling, like geraniums in July.

It holds my shadow in late afternoon, where I sit
beneath its latticework of branches.

I watch the ants criss-cross the bricks at my feet and envy
their progress – inherent, like pink hitting sky, foretelling night.

Their march of leaves goes on. Unlike us,
their reconstruction, unopposed.

If I stay here long enough the old Afghan gardener smiles
and brings me grapes.

I wonder – what does he think I miss the most?

His youngest boy walks by with a basket of bread,
bare feet scuffing in the sand and it's this –

the togetherness of his little toes,
the wholeness of his head and little wrist band,

his heels rough as salt
that cracks me like a watch face.

August

One hand on his head to keep him from sitting up,
his face flecked with foam – someone else's.
One hand on his wrist to keep tabs on his pulse.

For some reason I strain to hear it, confused
by the roar of the carrier backed up to the door
and the shouts and the shit stink
and the silhouettes of more wounded being brought in.

He asks – *Where's Brogue? How's Brogue?*

His breathing kicks in like a sob. He has half a pant leg
hanging off and one boot on, dangling,
his eyes fixed on the ceiling.

In that moment I can count each of his blinks,
the slow motion, open-close of his mind
replaying the whole thing – what he did
or should have done.

And I know Brogue's dead, not five minutes ago.
Only I don't tell him – instead I say, pausing,
that he did everything right.

Everything.

So now he knows.

And this time when I lay my hand on his head
he doesn't say a word – not one.

Naming the Sound that Took His Life

Ahmadullah.

Something like the whump of one
rotor blade, busting air

or jet afterburner caught
cupped in the hand

or cut short, a thunder clap
asphyxiating

its own wind.

Something like stillness in the mouth
or the spontaneous

combustion of leaves, a static

crackle of noise
that plumbs the deaf

eardrums like a sun
burst, blooming.

Then something like keening,
the awesome vowel of a mountain cave

calling and re-calling
the consonants of birds

dropped dead from a tree.

Notes on a Soldier

Shows me the carpets he bought.

Shows me his heart, or parts of –
the parts I haven't forgotten.

Admits to a daughter.

Runs like the wind,
but doesn't really bother.

Likes cats and kicking ass, hates being
behind the wire.

Shrugs a lot.

Displays fake breasts on his desk,
forgetting I'm there, then says

the days he's on a level
are just luck.

Car Bomb

There's a lock down in the middle of the day,
out by the arches at the eastern entrance to the city.

Afghan police receive word
that a suicide bomber is on his way.

Now every car left sitting by the side of the road,
every fruit cart and taxi cab is cause for alarm.

Backed off a bit in our row of trucks we have a good view.
There's not much else we can do.

The traffic piles up in the heat. Trunks get searched
and police in bad suits start waving them through.

We roll in slow, like a bead of sweat. Past the bleating of goats,
children in the back of a van, their hands
pressed up against the glass,

heat smouldering off every hood, cars hemming us in.
Beneath that hard blue sky – a sweltering

mile line of taxis that makes us know
we'll never know

which one's about to go up,

the one far enough away that we live
or the one close enough that we don't feel a thing.

Burying the Rabbit

At home her pet bunny dies.

Here, IEDS are unearthed,
find after find.

On the phone I try to talk to her, in between rockets
and thousands of miles away –

the connection is terrible. Her sobs
on delay. I have to keep saying –

Honey, what did you say?
What happened to the bunny?

I hate all this noise. I hate everything
but her voice.

She tells me Daddy is helping her
and hangs up. One hiccup

caught alone
at the end of the receiver.

Market Scarf

Red like leaves in the fall, you covered me
on a cot, inside a hot tent like a greenhouse
that turned sweat into shivers when night came.

You were that fragment of brick that the sun hits.

Then after we sent another one of our own
home in a box and I stayed up at night
among guys snoring in the dark –

you covered me as I wrote. And when I ran
on KAF's shit-coloured roads. One edge
wrapped around my mouth like a local
trying to keep the dust out.

You were an easy taste to acquire. Fire-coloured,
an RPG magnet inside the camp's wire. The guys
laughed and steered clear, asking –
weren't there any others?

It was hard to let it all go. I wore the smell of this place
far into your threads so I wouldn't forget
the feeling you kept

on my shoulders at night and how I stayed
awake until dawn, writing
metaphors for loss,
similes for red.

Rain

This evening, Afghan guards in their towers
come down for rain, barefoot like boys
laughing and throwing their hats,
rifles slung pointed down,
hot gravel caught in a downpour
that sends up dust in waves,
bathing our feet brown.

Plastic bags snap, flapping on the wire
and half-eaten apples get left, abandoned for rain
along the sandbagged tops of the wall.
All across the city it pours.
And me in my room on my last night,
shaking out my scarves, packing my clothes,
burning down my stores of brown sugar incense.
I watch its smoke drift out my door.
Watch the men out in the compound, laughing,
as it pours, rain flying up around their feet.

In my room with the screen door ajar,
I'm letting all the mosquitoes in,
staggering wet and dusty-backed,
incense dwindling
down to ash.

Afghanistan, on my last night –
rain so hard it danced.

Last Looks

I'm sitting with my back against a building
by the runway, kicking at my kit, anti-social as hell.
The sun is burning circles into my legs. I'm waiting
to get on the plane. I'm out of here for good.

I watch a newswoman on the tarmac
talk to troops about going home, their faces smiling,
heads nodding. I look away, sad
that I can't quite get there.

Still dwelling on suicide bombers and perfect paper sky,
this fight, both winnable and un-won,
the silence of mountains in the distance
plummeting, indivisible.

This morning the plane sits ready out on the runway,
its shadow rippling in the heat, its ramp folded down.

We head off towards it in single file.

My lungs go in and out like a last look.
I try to breathe it all in – all these hard things –
this detached ache like a paper kite on a cut string.

I can't figure out what it is I've lost.

Horizon Pool

Lounging poolside in Dubai on our way home,
I watch soldiers swimming, sun burnt and laughing
holding beer above their heads as they wade through the water.

They make jokes and the talk is mostly of tattoos or booze –
those nothing-to-lose conversations.

It's only later in the afternoon, when everyone is undone
by heat and the smell of chlorine evaporating on concrete
that guys on their backs, sweat pearled, smelling of coconut,
stop talking smack and turn to the one time
they each though they might die.

I lie on my stomach beside them. Unrelated families
at the far end of the pool splash and play. But at our end,
we are still, listening, each to our own thoughts

as the quiet fill of water spills from here to there, falling
off the edges of infinity – from one horizon to the next.

Masham Means Evening

Grapevine fires from beyond the hills in Arghandab
fill the land with smoke.

At sunset it comes drifting into camp,
smelling of pot.

Somewhere a coalition fire blazes, burning up
all the best hiding spots –

another offensive begins.

It's the end of the day in Kandahar. At the call to prayer
women in blue burqas wandering late through the bazaar,
hasten behind closed doors.

Wind carries land.

The sun sets into its own ash
and a man bikes quickly home.

Beneath the guard towers
emblazoned by the last rays of the sun –

one-eyed dog in a stone filled cemetery
prowls the pebbled mound of each new grave,
each one a tiny esker. The dog keeps vigil

beside the bombed out wreckage of an abandoned tank
inclined to a bed of rocks burned purple,

sits hunched on the ridgeline and watches birds circle
off the southern edge of the world.

He sleeps when night falls – one-eyed among the dead
and the stars described in arcs above our heads

too heavy to hold.

This is Masham.
Masham means evening.

Acknowledgements

None of this was done in isolation. For this reason I need to thank and acknowledge the following for their incredible personal and professional contributions to this experience – and this book.

To my team – you know who you are. Past, present, prodigals. You mean the world to me.

To those who have served and to those who continue serving – I'm honoured to be counted among you. I truly hope I've given us an accurate voice. To the fallen, to the families, to the wounded – inside and out – I'm humbled by what you have given, and what it cost. We're in your debt. Thank you.

To the entire team at Coteau Books – to Nik and Geoffrey – I'm so glad I knocked on your door. Thank you from my heart for answering. To my amazing editor, Elizabeth Philips – your insight and guidance were invaluable to me and both this book and my writing are far better for it.

And lastly, to the One who shuts the mouths of lions. I'd be nowhere without You.

"Man from Uruzgan" and "Disconnected" first appeared in *Prism International*.

"July in Brishna Kot," "Incoming" and "Naming The Sound That Took His Life," first appeared in *The Malahat Review*.

This manuscript was completed with the generous assistance of the Canada Council for the Arts.

About the Author

Kanina Dawson is the author of several works of literary non-fiction published in magazines such as *Event* and *subTerrain*. She has been awarded numerous prizes for creative non-fiction since 2001.

Masham Means Evening is Kanina's first published poetry collection and is based on her experiences while deployed as a serving member of the Canadian military in Afghanistan. Kanina lives and works in Ottawa.

ENVIRONMENTAL BENEFITS STATEMENT

By printing this book on FSC-certified recycled paper,
COTEAU BOOKS
ensured the following saving:

Fully grown trees	Litres of water	Kg of solid waste	Kg of greenhouse gases
1.18	4 343.35	65.79	171.02

These calculations are based on indications provided by the various paper manufacturers.

 Manufactured at Imprimerie Gauvin
www.gauvin.ca